MY AMERICAN KUNDIMAN

Also by Patrick Rosal

Uprock Headspin Scramble and Dive

MY AMERiCAN KUNDiMAN

POEMS
PATRiCK ROSAL

A KAREN & MICHAEL BRAZILLER BOOK
PERSEA BOOKS / NEW YORK

Persea Books, Inc.
853 Broadway
New York, NY 10003

Library of Congress Cataloging-in-Publication Data

    Rosal, Patrick, 1969-
    My American Kundiman : poems / Patrick Rosal.
        p. cm.
    "A Karen & Michael Braziller book."
    ISBN 0-89255-330-8 (pbk. : alk. paper)
    . Filipino Americans—Poetry. I. Title.

    PS3618.O774M9 2006
    811'.6—dc22

                    2006012910

Designed by Lytton Smith
Printed in the United States of America
First edition

For my life's most beloved strangers
—my grandparents—
Apolonio, Filomena, Alfonso, and Matilde

Acknowledgments

I'd like to acknowledge the following publications in which poems from this book first appeared:

"Meditations on the Eve of My Niece's Birth", *Vespertine*; "Ode to the Hooptie", *ABZ*; "About the White Boys Who Drove By a Second Time to Throw a Bucket of Water on Me", *Risen From East*; "Poem for My Extra Nipple", *North American Review*; "An Essay on Tango Composed While Listening to Adriana Varela", *Brevity: A Journal of Concise Literary Non-fiction*; "The Blue Room", "The Woman You Love Cuts Apples for You", *Boxcar*; As Glass", *Sow's Ear*; "The Boulevard Trilogy", *Pindelyboz*.

Special thanks to Michael Braziller, Karen Braziller, and to my editor and friend, Gabe Fried; Lytton Smith; Dinah Fried; Ross Gay; Curtis Bauer; Jon Wei; Thomas Lux; Joan Larkin; Suzanne Gardinier; Marie Howe; Joseph Legaspi; Sarah Gambito; Bino Realuyo; Lara Stapleton; Paolo Javier; Aimee Nezhukumatahil; Oliver de la Paz; Barbara Jane Reyes; Jon Pineda; Alex Socarides; Joe Weil; Roger Bonair-Agard; Marty McConnell; Lynne Procope; Mara Jebsen; Oscar Bermeo; Fish Vargas; Rich Villar; Eliel Lucero; Jessica Torres; the whole Louderarts crew; Jessica Hagedorn; Paul Genega; Chris White; Angela Conrad; Barbara Machtinger; Tom Slaughter; Sandy Van Dyk; Steve Golin; Ilona Anderson; Martie LaBare; Jeanne Nutter; Paul Puccio; Richard Hart; Glen Hayes; Paula Craig; all my colleagues and friends at Bloomfield College; Carleton Dunn; Nicole Dupree; Asheba Brown; Elaine Sexton; Aracelis Girmay; Leslieann Hobayan; Ron Villanueva; Tyehimba Jess; Luis Francia; Eileen Tabios; Bob Holman; Quincy Troupe; Tina Chang; Evelina Galang; Patricia Smith; Regie Cabico; Ishle Yi Park; Willie Perdomo; Krip Yuson; Steve Miller; the poets of Kundiman's summer retreat; my whole Jersey and NYC fam; Phil; E.; Jo-Jo; Junji; Janis; Anne; Monica; Chris; Ceez; Steve; G-mon; Tee; Doriega; Big Ben; Joel; Hex; Teej; Boodz; Atee; Trae; Melissa; Tia; Jose; Dennis D; Jay B.; Deez; Tony (aka Brigante); Kim; Ray; Rox; Richie; Jaymee; Chrissi; Honey; Jeff; Shaun; Mr. Michael Rose; Aige; Cleon; Wally; Steph; Marianne; Stunt; Rose A; Aiza; Joy; Jeremy; Chuck; Jeff; Lia; Harry J (aka DJ Dazz, aka Cubby); Jayvee; AJ; plus all the new additions; especially Nico; Marcus; Emmy; Christian; Annabelle; Brienna; and Remi. And with loving gratitude, most of all, to my dad, Tita Thelma, Christine, Anthony, Mark, Joe, Heidi, and Joyce.

CONTENTS

A Note on the Kundiman

The kundiman is a traditional Filipino song of unrequited love. Its name comes from the Tagalog phrase "kung hindi man," which, roughly translated, means "if you will not." Practice of the form changed during the Spanish colonial era and into the American occupation, as the woman about whom many kundiman were sung was not a woman literally, but the Filipinos' occupied homeland, a place with an increasingly ambiguous identity in the midst of violent erasure, fragmentation, and upheaval. The kundiman was a coded desire, a manifest longing in song, a beloved poetic subversion composed and sung in a time when overt expressions of love for the Philippines were looked down upon, if not completely prohibited by the nation's occupiers. Some of the poems that follow—and the spirit of the collection as a whole—mean to honor that tradition of kundiman. They are love songs for America.

ONE

Contigo

¿Mi tierra?
Mi tierra eres tú.

¿Mi gente?
Mi gente eres tú.

El destierro y la muerte
Para mí están adonde
No estés tú.

¿Y mi vida?
Díme, mi vida,
¿Qué es, si no eres tú?

—Luis Cernuda

With You

My country?
You are my country.

My people?
You are my people.

Exile and death
For me are where
You are not.

And my life?
Tell me, my love,
What is it, if it's not you?

—English translation by Curtis Bauer

Meditations on the Eve of My Niece's Birth

Who sow buckshot glitter from Cape May to Arthur Kill
Who weave rush-hour Kyrie from lanes of masonry
and steel Who stammer boldface gospel on Newark
subway steam What rot feed one man Who record
his rasp Who transcribe his song Who unknot his
gut What spectral redshift beacons ancient
boogie-on-down What heats the heart's
enthalpic pith Who stop the clock—
submit to speed of light When
have I listened—child—How
will I begin When shall I
open my mouth
and let half
the world
fall in

For Renata Mimi

On Our Long Road Trip Home I Don't Ask My Friend If He Thinks His Youngest Daughter Might Be Someone Else's Kid

The doe shudders a bit and the trucker
tells the woman who gored it with the front right bumper
of her late-model Chevy: *Your best bet next time*
is to hit the gas and slam full force into the fucking thing
Note to self: All things beyond logic are not
necessarily poetry The trucker draws his hunting knife
to slice clean the deer's jugular because he says
he can't take *it* anymore The *it* of his sentence
is probably as unclear to the trucker as it is to you
or to me or to Mikey who is telling me this story
on a ten-hour drive from the northern border
I like to think I'm doing my friend a favor by not mentioning
his two-year-old girl who laughs like him and shies away
from strangers just like her daddy does
though she looks nothing like him
and more like some handsome and nameless sucker
who invited Mikey's ex-wife out one night to wade naked
in the warm dark swamp of his crotch

I was about to make an argument for silence
and compare that silence to the trucker's knife
I was going to tell you it is a tool of mercy
and I was going to say quick sharp blades like that
are good for killing I could say all of that—but silence
isn't the knife and anyway I can't figure out
whose jugular to hack at or what suffering
creature I'd have to bloodlet first
or if we're simply better off slamming
full force into such gracile animals
Silence isn't Mikey or his dead mother
or the slut I make in my mind of Mikey's ex-wife
It is not even the vision of my own brother

lying down eyes closed on the Pulaski Skyway
inviting the fleet and heavy wheels of a sedan
over his fragile breast I'm thinking of that sudden
slender-bodied brute who rises from some
primitive and dreamless sleep and wanders
onto this boondock of an American interstate
staring into us late at night holding itself
steady before a two-ton rush of steel And still
my brother is not a deer and silence is not mercy
and I'm thinking of the mirth that trucker took
in finishing off a lame and bloodied mammal
and how neither Mikey nor I have the stomach
for the best of that sort of kindness which is to say
we are saving each other from the truth
and I'm doing my part when I jam the gas to the floor
headlong into the dull unlit road toward
the Jersey neighborhood neither of us wants to go back to
ready to make venison of the first swift beast
that dares to cross our path

Beast

They call him Beast where he's from and he will tell you
that each living physical moment *affords an opportunity*
to do something unique and beautiful Now clearly this is
bullshit You see I first became acquainted with Beast's
grunt-and-howl metaphysics at a dust-sucking
half-court game every Wednesday night in grad school when
on several occasions—yes—I stripped the ball from him
clean *Beautiful?* No—It was *ugly* And in the tradition
of the many monsters who came before him he did not cry
for such ugliness This Beast is six-foot-four and speaks
five versions of Pound-and-Pummel In South Philly
I'm watching him play summer league where Beast thinks
he's a poet even when he hauls down a brick
off the defensive boards and there's four other
black men on the court calling to him
Beast! Beast! Beast! He answers them
with all the sensitivity of a cretic foot: a quick
pivot mid-court that knocks the opponent's skinny
two-guard off the gawky pair of iron
skillets grown out of the poor kid's ankles and projects him
like an old neurosis across the crud-ridden gym floor
More than once I've caught Beast's blunt left wing-
blade of his broad back on my chin And then with my best
blacktop ineloquence cursed him: *Thank you Fuck you too*
Isn't this so often the affection between men
that we should share not a single lovely word unless
through a battered mandible This is how I listened to Beast
recite after those Wednesday nights his invented
names for fire in such holy brag and trash but also how
one morning over tea in a more muted bravado
he narrated the quiet trauma of his father's final weeks how
his old man—whose oak-switch cruelty Beast had long

survived—was shrunken down to a pair of scrawny wrists
How they yanked at the tethers to the gurney
with whatever will he could scrape from his gut
already nearing the end of its slow-cook to soup
Beast's father—conjuring one last good ass-whooping glare—
would shake his head pointing to his own mouth
He was signaling his son to remove the ventilator tube
shoved a full foot down his rotting neck Every nerve
in his failing body yowling soundlessly *No Not*
this I don't want this Take the goddamn thing out And Beast
dutifully answered the way any noble animal
must answer its closest kin: with his body With the dangerous
radius of his shoulders With his muscled trunk And with his breath
He watched the last of his father's silent wide-eyed squawks
and enacted a son's most loving disobedience
He held himself—for hours there—perfectly still

Tito's Field

Before Tito June began to ramble
    about the latest gorgeous prophecy
crackling in his Walkman swatting
    at the swift flies no one else could see
        this man—my uncle—was a genius

They paid him to figure out a way
    to suture kidneys shut when there
was none Then he'd go home
    to wreak his five-foot-nothing
        havoc on his sons and wife

And because the seven horsemen
    and their fairy counterparts
were quick to trample out my tito's
    last few lingering flintsparks of logic
        my auntie in the end stormed

out of their house with their sons
    the same way reason must have
stormed out of my uncle's brain But for one
    summer everyone and everything kept
        their tenuous residence long enough

for me to shoot guns in a field
    that belonged to my raving uncle
somewhere in the middle of Louisiana
    Tito June explained each weapon's
        caliber and range He even knew

the physics of every echoed *Blam!*
  My aim was terrible
I was just a Jersey kid drunk
  on the triple-jump twenty-gauge
    cuss and rumble of a shotgun

thrumming its way out of that
  seventeen-acre field in a hurry
When he told me to knock one fat grackle
  off the lowest branch of a bare catalpa
    about forty feet from where we stood

I surprised myself when I hit the bird
  and saw the body drop still fluttering
Tito June pulled a .22 off his hip
  walked up to the final full
    twitch that remained of the bird

and sent a slug through its tiny gut
  When he picked it up and held it by one
toe dangling it like an iridescent planet
  I knew he'd pack that one away
    with all the other critters in his freezer

Maybe some of you are thinking I should thank him
  —my genius Tito June who cackled loud
when he pulled a trigger cackled loud
  when he didn't Yet for all his quirky brilliance
    for all his ravishing lunacy and

universe-be-damned bravado I don't
    envy him his dreams: their gunblast
echoes rippling through the field
    of his mind: littered tangled overgrown
        where every day he stands gaping

about to pronounce some twisted epistle
    or botched psalm on the verge of a world
where there is no such thing as lies and chaos
    will be the only science
        he shall ever love

Etude #8, Modéré

When his father died the thirteen-year-old Villa Lobos
began to scuttle through the roughhouse streets of Rio
with—legend has it—a borrowed guitar
Excoriated by his mother for wanting to play music
instead of studying germs and bones
he spent his nights imitating on six strings
an entire city Not just the swift-fisted pimps
and the hot batucada of vendors but the light
bounding off the gray irises of a blind man
the nuns' plump asses switching in the afternoon heat
the marooned look of some Saturday penitent
fingering a bead's smooth black skin

Okay so I've made this up: the blind man
and his gray eyes the rrrah-tah-teh-pang
of Brazilian vendors the pimps the penitent
and our sexy nuns All of it false except
a mother's bereavement and her sneak of a son
learning to listen through his very groin
to the romp odors throughout his native city
its zigzag hollers and cucurru cascades
chiming down the avenues This is how he deceived
his widowed mom only to stay out all hours
jamming to Rio's angelic lusts Maybe sometimes
we discover something small about anguish
by one hand's length splayed out stretched
to its limit just to unlock a metropolis of aches

If you think this is the story of a man making
a city of his music you must know it is also
the story of a city composing a man: the subtle
accidentals of his elbows his eyes' deep

fermata the vast tacet measures of grief left
in one father's wake In theory you might
call it a rest and if you listen carefully
you might hear in those naughty
hip-grinding melodies the almost caroled contrabasso
of his dead papa and the paltry alto of young Heitor
nearly speaking back to so stark and fresh
an emptiness with a joke or some prayer...
or with a silence which is itself nearly a song
and that itself—beloved cousin—is nearly enough

For a friend who is learning to play guitar

Greed

I deserve nothing but rivers
     stirred in ginger
          the Ganges swept west
your mother's tit
     I'll take a beggar's dime
          I'll take his stagger
I'll take burlap and cashmere
     the slack rope of bound-up
          barges & yachts
I'll take minnows & caviar
     palmshacks & mansions
          I'll open your sister's
mouth Watch me
     take away her breath

Lapu Lapu's Envoy Conveys His Response to Magellan

> "The teachings of history show that to send a score or so of Europeans in coats
> of mail against a thousand naked slaves, Indians, or what not, armed with
> fish-bone lances, was by no means absurd...A few gunshots, a few shrewd
> blows, and Silapulapu's poor fellows would be on the run like hares."
> —*Conqueror of the Seas: The Story of Magellan*, Stefan Zweig

Anger—you sonofabitch—is but one god and gods require
men to pray: to hold in their lungs some old nameless ghost and distend
their puny human chests with it 'til they damn near break then merely bend
down as if their backs have been whacked raw with rattan before their own pyre

What do you know of the twenty-one tempests we can conjure
with a kiss How our saints bless our barbs with venom How we'll deify
your scrawny handsome messiah (He will love us too will teach us to defy
you who rattle the blue belly of heaven) If not with power

then with craft and ken will we coax you to our shores kill you and plant
—beside the stained brackish waters—your pale spear-pocked remains
And the god of salt who is the god of love and labor will mend
my brave soldiers' blood with your own Traitor... Christian... sycophant

May this god of anger who is the god of fear with both eyes closed give
me the wits to release him quickly May he grant me the grace to disbelieve

Some Questions About the Garden for a Friend Two Years Out of Prison

There's a garden and the fruits' dull thud
and the question I'm asking: if
you'd bite the apple
or give it back to your only
love and watch her walk out into desert and toil
alone would you give back that infraction
and every wince at sin to follow: seven days
in solitary after the screws
told you to stomp a rapist
to bloody mince Would you give back your arm's
burnmark—by brother
or not—the knife you stuck
into a man's side the chains
the bricks the sweet beat-
downs and Chinatown windows stung
by thugs Would you give back
the song you thought you'd hum till dawn
squatting in a thornbush
'til the cops went home
and what about the light the sudden buzz
outside the cell across your prison block
Would you behave stay-put shutdown
and no one rush to see what's up that night
but you what of the man there
Would you give him back too the one
who's pissed and shit his pants
head cocked dangled wrapped
in a bedsheet from his cell's ceiling
angels given up on his wrists' strings
Would you give back the alarm you rang
to call the guards to haul him—barely
breathing—out would you hand all that back

Would you lure from their tombs
the lately dead fuming of toilette
You say you love the old the broke-down
the sorry beasts of East London
Would you give it back
I'm askin' Blood Would you eat
the fruit Would you want to live long enough
to never speak of it again

A Poet Visits with Prisoners

I smuggle steam
and the funk of an unbathed woman
who's left early from my bed

These things are better
than fiction but I carry lies with me
as well: one in each hand

and several between my teeth
This is how I've learned
to let murderers

touch me
I touch them too
I hold their elbows when we embrace

They do not cry
And they're not waiting 'til I leave
They describe the scent of apples

It's how they teach me to be free

Filipino Cats Circa 1999

They who stalked
dancefloors on hind legs

bucket cap tilt
to one side sipped

slow from a bowl
hopped from barstool

to barstool They three
gun-cocked brothers

nine lives each
Smooth quick keen

seers in the dark
always landing feet first

even the youngest one
who jumped

from seven stories up

Playing Congas with King David at My Brother's Wedding

Me and this David are an angel's full flight from hell's char
and half-way to heaven's chin I'm sweating hard from the biblical
fevers that first burned these skies black that tripped the funky spark
that flamed polyrhythmic
                                    I can almost trace my own frail umbilical
light to those topsy turvy heavens The stars' dimmed gab
keeping an ancient time They hold watch They blaze like soldiers loyal
to the order of agonies to our generation of ghosts to this happy mob
found in tonight's simmer and bliss (Isn't joy too a kind of broil)

For ten days my palms will bruise as though I've learned to incur
the bluest singe of the oldest fires Music—that ancestral heat—heckles
despair and we lust for such hot thrumming
                                    —this king and me—we slur
and sweat and mock tonight how vast our common sorrow We jackal
what tenderness we can Tonight we shall grow old
                                    We shall toast to our heels
God will fling us back to sea & we'll jam
                                    'til we spit salt up from our gills

When You Haven't Made Love in a Long Time

Whatever first summons back her mouth
to yours—gin or lies or the massive electric
wreck of an old man's heart Whatever rouses
your clumsy pulse to its blessed hectic

measures Whatever lusty villain's
vague halo or blissless wrist you mimic
Whatever thoracic harbor your passions thrill in
Whatever ash and lye Whatever fragrant muck

lets your tongue be neither simple nor mad-dash
without knowing first the ramshackle
angles of angels rising Do not rush
from *if* to *yes* Travel a gentle sickle

Climb her thigh's solfeggio Hush along her hips like
some cool crooning devil eager to lose his wits

The Woman You Love Cuts Apples for You

and stirs them in sea salt and vinegar
She takes a drag from her Silk Cut

eases again through the fruit's flesh
the blade stopping short of her thumb

You are both sweating at the shoulder
(East Ham's hottest summer) And you realize

these are not the times to come to poetry
You have everything you need

Your father's bone-hard stare
can't reach across the Atlantic

so you save yourself for another day
because there is this woman slicing apples

stirring them in vinegar reminding you
of an afternoon twenty-five years ago when

you knelt with your brothers at your mother's
feet to pluck apple slices from a small basin

pinched between her legs And one of you
would lift that bowl—almost completely empty

except for a sour clouded liquid
and a few seeds shifting at the bottom

You'd just taste at first but soon you're handing it
from brother to brother gulping lung-fulls

of that tart cider You'd sweat sniffle gasp chug
'til your lips turned white and numb

And before you went out into those Jersey streets
you'd rinse your chin You'd soap your hands

because the girls would hold their breath
for every reason and stink on your fingers and neck

You won't dare tell anyone you've learned
to love the taste of something so strange until this

woman cuts apples for you in vinegar
and the familiar fumes fill your nostrils and gullet

She will lift the bowl to drink She'll twist her face
and laugh when she offers it and you will drink

and she will drink and you will drink again
She will kiss your cut knuckle She'll kiss your eyes

Of course the vinegar stings
It's the hottest summer ever in London

And you and the woman you love fall asleep side by side
like this—reeking and unwashed—breathing in

each other's dreams of open skin

An Essay on Tango Composed While Listening to Adriana Varela

I swear to you I heard someone on Avenida Santa Fé shout my name but I ignored it Who knew me in this city anyway? I'd come here trying to forget the woman whom I'd made love with every night for three weeks in another August in another city whose once-in-a-lifetime dog-licking summer stewed the hot copper reek of coins right out of my palms But in this city I put my head down as I walked thinking of that story about the boy who remembered everything: every swelter of ascent every susurration of fire every etymology of touch

I didn't get very far before I heard that voice shouting my name again This time I stopped to turn around and saw a woman selling flowers A thin dress No makeup I thought even if one day she should grow old you wouldn't doubt she was once very beautiful She was looking straight at me and shouted again *Patricio*! Clearly now she was looking at me I just stood there and she stood there too and because it was winter it should have been cold but we stared at one another with all the foot traffic eddying about us and maybe it was only a few seconds (on a crowded avenue they call Faith no less) before I twisted away and headed back to my Recoleta flat to get on with my forgetting and fail

If like me you don't know well the cruel music of tango then you don't know how its truths can haunt you—haunt you like a strange city and a strange woman shouting for you on a crowded avenue haunt you like a late languish for too few afternoons sipping from the smooth shell of a shoulder like coming back to where you've lived your entire life and then having no idea where you are going It is the kind of song that will make you beg Gardel to reinvent your fool breath—and he will

Because a beautiful woman once broke my heart without trying I've spent long stretches of my life perfecting one amnesia after another and I'm telling you someone is shouting my name on Avenida Santa Fé She is calling from that lovely nowhere and when a woman sings for you like that how will you wander wherever you wish alone How will you not want to go back to kiss her and have her taste an entire river's silver soaked in the shallows of your bones

Soneto Para Encontrarte

I will wake up in a foreign city and walk
each morning with no direction no map
no guide only a few kind citizens chatting
endlessly about gallows and brass I will talk
until the air tastes like meat and whiskey
and the brisk step of beggars won't wake me
to the short canons of desire each voice counterpoint
to a coin's winter sting each sour note a ducat
paying my crawl toward the first dying the first
'O' the first swig and chug of grief
                                    So when
a woman holds my face between her knees—her child
already dreaming of a father suddenly gone—I will kneel
and murmur she will arch and wheel and I
will eat and drink like this 'til holy kingdom come

Dear Aracelis

Today's storm is
so hard and lovely
under the thunder's frantic
gunmetal kickback under
this gargantuan whisper
of rain that I'm walking
past Rahway's silver
maples just starting
to nudge their April
nubs into the city's grime
and I want to pluck
one of those tender buds
and place it in my mouth
then walk downtown
among the ashy vagrants
and big black dudes
smoking Cubans
and playing chess
knowing not one of them
will have a clue
I got the end
of an entire winter
between my teeth
like the time in London
I stole a plum from the tree
where Keats wrote
his nightingale and I
promised I wouldn't eat
that sour knuckle
but popped it anyway
into my mouth
And for three days

I sucked every
bit of flesh off it
till all was left was the pit
and I swore I could taste
that city's every conflagration
and soot and I held that
on my tongue too
even as I kissed
my Baby goodbye
and I wasn't even
ready to go home
and Aracelis I've survived
every mayhem so far
between that plum pit
and this silver maple bud
I'm holding now
on my tongue: the end
of an entire winter
about to discharge itself
into the gargantuan whisper
of rain and this bastard
summer starting only
now to burn and burgeon
against the inside
of my cheek

Two

Kundiman

Ang sabi mo pula ang paborito mo.
Ang sabi ko puti ang paborito ko.
Kagabi nang tayong dalawa'y nagkita,
nakapula ako at nakaputi ka.

—Emmanuel Lacaba

What you said was red is a favorite of yours.
What I said is white was a favorite of mine.
When the two of us saw each other last night,
I dressed in red and you wore white.

—English translation by Paolo Javier

Kundiman In Medias Res

and I like sometimes to begin
in the middle of things
your breastbone/navel
the small of your back
your hand's syntax pausing
at the comma of my thumb
I love your 700 questions
each strand curled long
across my lips the sudden
punctuation of your spine
Your mouth an interrogative
sliding from unknown
to unknown They say
one sign leads to another
I say each tastes vaguely
like blood Along my body's
broken lines I am still unwritten
by your fingers' calligraphy

Love—decipher me
Speak me with your first tongue

Kundiman on a Dance Floor Called Guernica

Don't push me 'coz I'm close to the edge
I'm tryin' not to lose my head uh huh huh huh huh
—Ed Fletcher (a.k.a. Duke Bootee)

This woman and I are watching the b-
boys contort cocksure

swagger into dance Down
to the very ligament their bodies

are wattage their names writ in whiskey
and smoke their legs scribbling

into the room's boned twilight
a gospel according to Duke

These dancers are thunder's bastards
And at the borders of their human maelstrom

a woman's hips are winding their own
slow vortex between my hands

We twist time with our waists
Each sweat-slick bass note hangs

in the room like a heavy bruise
healing its way to another storm

I am losing my hands to her
I am learning to drown

above water
But make no mistake

We think we are not in love
And no one can hear us

We are moaning for each other's air

Kundiman in which a B-Boy Contemplates How Rome (Like Many Fallen Cities) Was Not Built in a Day

but you ruin me
—in other words—

in just one You rouse
my blunder-struck

tongue stall
my systolic

boom-bap heart
to a knee-deep

drone You sunder
hard from stone

Baby sometimes I want
you to kiss me in lethal

doses Love me 'til
the morning stink

Bless me with pan-
demonium In other

words: Wreck me
to travertine

tufa and brick
Demolish me

a metropolis Burn me
down the Babylon

for which my whole
body
        breaks

Kundiman: Offering

sacrum   this holy bone
      addiction/benediction
in the same
         tree
           burning
     to say
         at their root

Kundiman Ending on a Theme from T La Rock

Your morning's
everyday stained
caul of exhaust Your
plum bludgeoned
dusk Your fine
stench and luck-
less French kiss
Your can-I-get-
down bliss Your god-
gone blesséd
Jones for loam
Your Jersey baroque
Your Mercy
9's sirens prying
every sky Your
name Your flow
Your funk Your every-
day nasty Your very
revelry Your break-
neck scat the loot
you boost Your
rags Your seven-
thousand-island
slang Your hype
Your hips Your spit
Your sickest wit
and snip Your every
severed syl-
lable Your blunt-
toke fables Your
smoke's reprieve
Your lever's

torque bearing your
body every
day Every lovely
mucking hum
Your mic sound
nice Every Check
One Your
fade Your cut
Your knife Your
jazz on-two Your bass
Your every clef Your
left breast Your
folly Your lung
Your modest rot
Your alibata
tongue Do you want it
(*Hell yeah!*) baby—
'cause it's yours

Anthem Kundiman Blue

We might have some bad taste in shoes
        but we sneak around just fine
Me and you take their name in vain
        when they have us drink a little brine

Love let's creep again into their tabernacle
        Let's strip down to our knees
Let's sing in two voices one funky hymn
        and make love next to their shrine

Kundiman: The Good Bite

                    She is
the good bite
                    the long noon
a stiff lick of whiskey
on the lips
               She speaks
a chest's muted
syn-
        copations
and bare tooth
                    on stone
a storm's adagio
                    conjured
at finger's tip
She is the good
                    bite—
the one whose touch
[like the numb
                    rush
of a drug
        to your vein] will
break
        your heart
                    in whole

Kundiman: Tarsus

The night I held a candle to your feet
you said   I was about to fall in love   I dreamt this   I dreamt
my fingers became the light across   your ankle   rising
            along your thigh   fading there
And while the alpha bulls at the bar   locked horns
and while the other boys   took turns   paying the big blind
and while this is still   America   and
Shakespeare is dead and Lady   Day is dead and Biggie and Tupac
dead   YOU   *are about*   *to fall in love*   you said
            And knowing you as little as I did
you must have been composing in your head some kind of poem
I dreamt this too   In that darkening room
        me and the boys   folded one by one   our hands
And I watched you a while   through a clear bottle of rum
and started to whisper your name into it   —no—*through* it
            saying each syllable   slow
as I tapped their rhythm on the glass   with a spoon   listening
to those gentle velar repetitions refracted   back
                        into my ears like drowned strings
        to hear their fragile dactyls hum
a sort of prayer: the name of a woman
who would not dare   dream me back to light   to that meager bone
            we almost coaxed a little burning from

Kundiman for My Lover Beside Me on the Floor
(Her Daughter Asleep on My Bed)

There are things I would like to know
right now: a woman's left hip called morning
her right hip called night
and the secret blossom between
slowly becoming dusk
how long to hold the anaphora of breath
along her sternum Every day I say
Tell me what you like and every day you say
it's your daughter's fingers twirled in your hair
Once it was the calluses of my hands
Tonight you sleep beside me
as though this is practice for the only way
you know to say goodbye

I've wanted to mistake your eyes for sadness
I've wanted to kiss the wings
tattooed on the back of your neck
to know your belly by its quiver I've wanted
to touch your breast like a man
learning his name in Braille Maybe then
I thought I'd sleep for once without the dream
of being lost in the landscape of your lap
waiting for you to tell me where I am
as if I could find my way back
as if I had some idea of home
as if I could ever live
where my heart was not ashamed to break

THREE

I would curse you in Waray, Ilocano, Tagalog, Spanish, English, Portuguese, and Mandarin; I would curse you but I choose to love you instead.

—from *Dogeaters* by Jessica Hagedorn

Poem for My Extra Nipple

Burnt-out sun shut eye
still-born amoeba
miniscule miscarriage
of the flesh ant head
desiccated heart
a volcano's embryo
unborn twin budged
through my breast misplaced
knuckle I let my woman
kiss me here: this
brown pearl of Olongopo
Bay thorn pierced
inch-deep into dermis
milkless gland
the aria's last note
lost between armpit
and sternum It is a secret
passage to the aortic
contortions behind my ribs
swollen sand grain
from the beach where
I watched my brother
nearly drown
—I pray to it—
the singed hint
of some great-great
grandfather's sin
come back

About the White Boys who Drove By a Second Time to Throw a Bucket of Water on Me

> "...there shall never be rest
> 'til the last moon droop and the last tide fail..."
> —Arthur Symons

The first time they merely spat on me and drove off
      I stood there a while staring down the road
   after them as if I were looking for myself
         I even shouted my own name
But when they cruised past again
    to toss a full bucket of water
  (and who knows what else) on me
         I charged—sopping wet—after their car

and though they were quickly gone I kept
      running Maybe it was hot that August afternoon
   but I ran the whole length of Main Street past
the five-and-dime where I stole Spaldeens
        and rabbits' feet past the Raritan bus depot
    and Bo's Den and the projects where Derek and them
  scared the shit out of that girl I pumped
      the thin pistons of my legs all the way home

Let's get real: It's been twenty-five years
    and I haven't stopped chasing them
  through those side streets in Metuchen
      each pickup b-ball game every
swanky mid-town bar I've looked for them
    in every white voice that slurred and cursed me
  within earshot in every pink and pretty
      body whose lights I wanted to punch out

—and did To be honest I looked for them
        in every set of thin lips I schemed to kiss
    and this is how my impossible fury
            rose: like stone in water I ran
all seven miles home that day and I've been
        running ever since arriving finally
    here and goddammit I'm gonna set things straight

The moment they drove by laughing
    at a slant-eyed yellowback gook
            they must have seen a boy
who would never become a man We could say
        they were dead wrong but instead let's say
    this: Their fathers gave them their rage
            as my father gave me mine

and from that summer day on we managed
        to savor every bloody thing
    that belonged to us It was a meal
            constantly replenished—a rich
bitterness we've learned to live on for so long
        we forget how—like brothers—
we put the first bite in one another's mouths

For My Childhood Friend Derek who First Told Me I Could Call Him Nigger

I don't know when

the white kids in our neighborhood got permission to use it
or how they figured it was safe for them to say around me—for I wasn't

one: Not dark enough—I mean—to scare their mothers yet not cracker
enough to date their sisters Know this: I didn't think of you as black

until the day you said I could call you nigger You meant to say we were
brothers So know this too: Since that day I have shouted this word inward

and let it echo throughout the dim continent of my skull I have split it open
with my bare hands like a plum and sucked its purple juice from my thumbs

I have cut it up into eleven pieces rigged its razored gears fermented it
in my spleen to gin and razed whole fields with it by blaze What shouldn't

a yellow boy like me know about a noun doused in 500 years of burning
What could I do when you poured its fire into my palms and said *Take this*

Drink And when did I learn to say it proud as a white boy How did I put it then
to my lips How easy to love the turn of a single word's blade cutting

every which way at once

As Glass

When the sons of Buenos Aires holler
in chorus from the muck-blessed soccer field

across the street they are calling to me
in the formal idioms their fathers use

to ignore the ubiquitous feral dogs
and the beggars of Recoleta

I understand just enough to fling
back halfway to the park's paved border

their summer-toughened leather ball
and return to my hardfloor Palermo flat

to phone my dad back in Jersey: *Papa* I say
Tu hijo habla Of course at first he doesn't

recognize my voice or even his own name
for I am speaking to him with an affection

whose prepositions point in all the wrong directions
but for six full minutes we are unfamiliar

with one another's rage For once
we are laughing at the same time

It's simple: we don't loathe one another in Spanish
like we do in English—a language I've long known

for its fluid burn The way it rises from my father's
ankles into his belly from his torso into his limbs

like molten glass This is why he and I
can glare at one another for decades

without moving—all the lexicons
of sadness and delight turning cold and hard

about every muscle and bone twisting
around the capillaries flooding the metacarpal nooks

stopping in the esophagus So if flesh sinew and gut
(this human crucible) were to fall away—as it must—

what's left is the clear anatomy of a man
cast in language unsummoned for 77 years:

the whittled wooden fans of his childhood
his mother's kalesa rocking over Vigan cobblestone

a whore's warm breasts flushed against him
like a good bottle of rum cracked cathedral windows

some cots and soup and all 400 years of horse shit
poured hot through his veins And I

am there too—sitting in a chilly apartment in Palermo
listening to the fading howls from the football field

the bold charity of a foreign tongue sweetening
the image in my mind of this quickly aging man who

whacked me and my brothers silly with his leather belt
And down the street I can still hear those boys

teasing one another in lunfardo Maybe they're not too young
to despise their fathers Maybe they can already taste

in the prayers they pretend to say before they sleep
that petty venom distilling in their mouths But not today

Not in this Castillian For today this speech
of imperial thieves this dialect of conquerors this

larcenists' parlance I am taking back
as my own and every word of every tenderness

I have failed to speak is already rising through my knees
as glass It is ancient and it is pure It is not free

of bitterness or grief It is heating
my very fingers as I write this: I want to learn

to love more fluently even if it means in English
I should shatter into the body of my father

St. Patrick

After the man
they say chased
the snakes
out of Ireland
after the patron of the day
my father was ordained
into the Church
he wanted me
baptized
with a word
clicked shut
like a trap My name
starts with the brittle
snap of kiln-
dried wood and ends
with a trick It claims
my skin my flat
nose thick lips
the eleven ways
I've kissed one
woman to sleep

When I die
I want my friends
to christen me again
dab my head
with oil bless
my lips with rum
I want them to give me
a name they'll tag
in alleys chisel
into rock cracked

in its side
a name as far
from heaven as the next
George Street bar
I want a name like
a Luther Vandross
slow jam like
a kundiman like
a New Orleans doubletime
march something
they can pour
on the floor
stomp on
with their shoes
grinding it
to dust I want them
to dance
till their god-
forsaken feet
turn blue

The Blue Room

That was the year I first smelled a girl
on my fingers—a consensus of sweat and blood
and bloom—the same year a skinny Polish kid and me
turned a recess tussle into a year-long fight
not long after I learned "Hotel California" on the guitar
and squeaked a desperate chorus to every
freckled schoolyard chick who'd listen
That was the first year I believed the white boys
who bragged about all the sex they'd had It seemed
everything by then was a race so there I was still
crouched at puberty's starting blocks anxious
to sprint toward that orangutan manhood of my own
Each afternoon at the library across the street
from St. Francis Convent where nuns without
last names came and went (the ones who taught us
to memorize the seven gifts of the Holy Spirit and
to avoid the only two kinds of sin that mattered—
mortal and fun) Carrie Anne Jean and I
would loiter between stacks of big-print novels and
artbook nudes reclined in some French meadow
We hid behind racks of *Boy's Life* and *Highlights*
finally crept upstairs to an empty lights-out
high-ceiling high-windowed vault of a space
where everything gave up its color
for some vague shade of blue
where she and I jammed our tongues
into each other's mouths—more lost than lustful—
where I lifted her plaid skirt and she goose-stepped
out of her panties and I pulled down
her bra to taste her nipples pink and perked
between my lips Of course
I didn't *want* to—I *had* to
What could be more Catholic

Sometimes I wonder what's become of that
strong-thighed half-French/half-Irish gymnast who let me
for one year in the Blue Room of the public library
slowjam and slopkiss her from neck to hip—two of us
dodging the few beams of afternoon that lit
the slant columns of dust our bodies unsettled until
we emerged into the full light back
downstairs to the other kids: her friends in one corner
and the white boys in another waiting hungrily
to sniff the what-was-it-like musk of my hands
and inhale from my fingers the perfume of a future
they swore they already knew

Ode to the Hooptie

This is for those cars—early model
part rust/part primer a patch
of clear coat still holding on
to the bumper—chugging mid-day
down I-95 packed to the rear
window: milk crates blankets books
Someone in there is determined
to move on This is for those cars—
out of state—squeaking smoky
side-swiped towed broken into
The deep scrape on the driver's side
door The flapping plastic window
and taped brake light Hunk
of metal plastic & glass It goes
at its own pace It's made it this far

Tito Teddy with a Cigarette Dangling from His Mouth Uses My Arm to Illustrate a Jiu Jitsu Bone-Break Move from His Coast Guard Days

The Ship—the Dallas—oh
man it's like a cruise ship Big big
fucking thing You can't see
no pipes You know what I mean? Real
nice It got the TV and everything So
this white guy—right? Tall—
like six-four—skinny
but tall—this white guy—man—
he gave this little Filipino guy
a black eye Then he turns to me
(calls me a name—a monkey
or something like that
This is the old days You
know) I say *I don't got nothing*
with you Why you gonna fight me for
And he says *Get over here you*
summonabitch And you know
we learned a little boxing
from this black guy—a little bit:
have a jab footwork Gotta
have good feet And you know
when he jab you just
move your head a little
like that PAH! You move just
a little like PAH! And that's what I did
—y'know? He took me outside
We out on the dock Hrmph—
Big goddamn white guy And
all o'dem other guys
on the deck Officers too Even
the CPO Everybody
is watching You know what I mean?

So when I shake his hand
—y'know—I take his elbow
and *crrack* it—like that But
you gotta be quick—crack!
And he try to jab but
he got only one arm now
so when he jab back I move my head
just a little and PAH!
like that puh-PAH!—y'know?—
Everybody watching
I *break* that guy's arm
I beat up that summonabitch
Those were the days Shit
He never mess with me again

Two Black People and a Filipino Near the Concessions Stand at the Geraldine R. Dodge Poetry Festival

It wasn't bad the man held back your fries
and asked if you'd already paid It wasn't bad
me you and Nic had just enough money
to get us home trying to buy for the three of us
one large lemonade (no ice with two extra cups)
And it wasn't bad a drink cost one
half of what each of us had that day and 1/10
of everything we owned *No* we conferred beside
the food stand about our lack of bank when
a woman in an Eddie Bauer vest asked
Are you on line You shook your head No
And she said: *Thank God I didn't want
to be killed or anything*
                                    How long the pause
before we realized we didn't all hear
the same thing wrong How long then before
the three of us bust into laughter from
disbelief almost fallen forward
rolling in Jersey dirt till our guts knotted like
a Ha-Ha-Oh-Shit-God-damn giddy rot let loose
in our bellies How long Dunny

The next time some motherfucker asks if
you already paid you can tell him *Over
and over for 400 years* You can tell him
you got a wife and four kids and you write
poems Matter of fact you can tell him *Man
give me that side of fries two cokes
for my friends plus forty-one
acres and a mule*

For Asheba, Nicole, and Carleton

-55-

On Behalf of My Teenage Nephew: A Humble Supplication to Sadness

When this six-foot beautiful hooligan
is drugged cuffed and dragged
back to the Center for Living (a ten-room hospital ward
with three steel doors locked both ways) it will keep him
a few days from his cramped quarters at home
where he stalks back and forth in some imagined cage
threatening to bash his daddy's head open
with a bat I want to know: What useless
art will save him now? I once heard
In order to have happiness you must
pay your debt to sorrow Well
even if it's true the heart's got such bullshit
bureaucracies such careful accounts of this and that
Do not exact right away the full rotten fine: let him
wail all night all day and through another
yet again From the fulcrum of his hips
let him rock his every petty
misery—with his handsome body you might mistake
for laughter's scabbard Let it be the sweetest keen
a thug can cut into the air from lip to crotch Let him sob
Let him shell out every hour of nineteen years
and then some—I mean yes let him square
his mother's lien as well I mean appraise it
in his sopping sleeves and knees Dear Anguish
—my spoiled chum—I'm asking you
to bear away two lifetimes-worth
what he owes But don't truck all at once
—you greedy bastard—the whole stinking due Let him learn
to carve slowly into his lap with a weeping
the heat and weight of molten silver the names of those
he can barely stand to love and let
every letter burn across his belly Then

call your accruals nil Cull from his old age
your skimpy tariffs so this exuberant bully and I
will have a chance or two to earn from one another
the proper wages of men so we might scrawl
our corrected ledgers into the margins
without aching for some familiar sorrow
to set us and our fathers free

For CJ

Crossfade (from *DJ Krazee Bladez' Collectio Rituum*)

This morning the sound of one brother smacking
　　another floats down from a second-story window
　　　　like a flock of birdless wings: a handclap cadence
　　summoned from some dapper gypsy gremlin crooning saetas
　　　　into a church-organ blues a penultimate harmony
　　　　　　an imperfect fifth which fades finally but holds long
　　　　enough to lift and plunge again under the hallelujah
　　chord of a northbound horn wound above a train where
　　　　this boy spits hi-hats into his hands like prayer
　　　　　　kicks too and scratches and snares dropping them
　　　　over the *Amen* reprise of the tracks' seams *Amen*
　　Amen between their *Bloom Dig-uh Blash* refrain
Amen Amen between backbeat and beatback *Amen*

Boulevard Trilogy

I. How Boulevard Lost His Mind

Boulevard was tired of all the slow birds in his brain: the awkward leaden ones with lazy plumage and ponderous toes They were rude painful and fat They had little eyes Their sloppy tongues lapped him up in a noxious drool So one day he swatted one to the corner and replaced it with a quick and lovely swallow How it flit and soared and seemed to be many places at one time The swallow danced and dove with its mouth open taking into its little belly whole throat-fulls of his mind's sky It lived on the swaths of heaven left blank by the torpid bird which Boulevard thought he had rid himself of

They say the sky will double at least once during a man's lifetime and so it did in Boulevard's head But turgid birds came three by three and then some to fling themselves about So he swatted them away too To fill the aching gapes of heaven he invited another swallow then two then three (their flashy undersides a dazzle and distraction) then nuthatch then murderbirds then uncountable dozens more This is how he thought he'd save himself but soon enough his whole brain had become a madness of wings A squeaky starling racket Grackles darkening him to a translucent blue Pigeons fucking on the rooftops Maimed gray swans And those first swift birds—still slamming themselves against cranial walls until his skull filled up And this is how Boulevard lay down his head—all heavy with pretty corpses and the dread

II. The Ghost of Boulevard's Mother: Trick

In the kitchen which is no longer my kitchen I select the blade choose the fruit hear the chopping board clap against the counter I want the aftersting of shrimpaste ginger salt I slice a ripe bittermelon lengthwise to scoop the seeds I cut the middle bit and feel the dull push of the knife against my skin and see the nick fill with pink and swell I'll catch a glimpse of me—a wince against the fading light and the trick of the eye a figment of fish and steam The woman who cooks here now who lies in my husband's bed she says my name at night She's half awake shuddering like a feverish child except the heat in her forehead and hands—the burn between her legs—is me I enter her the way night floods an empty jug Sometimes I find myself in her wrists as she brushes her hair from her eyes I feel her breasts weighing heavily to one side or another I can almost get up and walk almost leave my husband breathing deeply—twitching I can nearly find my way to the kitchen blind I am in her throat and on her tongue I ride the breaths that pass between her lips So when she says my name—I am almost speaking again

III. To Boulevard Waking

Yes it troubles me: the way morning comes on giving up its bright belly how the shadows' edges cut the streets into a dagger's angles It's not midnight or the heat of high noon that I have come to love It's the nine minutes that aren't night—aren't dawn—after an evening of little sleep when I dream of beating senseless a stranger who will not drop until I take a crowbar or axe to his shoulder and still he won't stay down It's in a place I keep calling home—but I don't even know where to find the closest door

And there's always a woman who comes along She's resurrected from the dead She smells of gardenia which reminds me of a Spanish name and the woman she is always coming back to life like this: reanimated from seaweed and brush—sugar cane and stone One time I remember she had a limp and a long scar down her left arm She was singing—no words really—and no melody It was a falsetto she hummed to me as a child—a glissando lost in heat and glass It's the morning—when I think I got nothing to keep me—no memory of anguish no harm to my teeth or hazard to my knees—alive and I'm wrong I have nine minutes and I have the stranger I have the strange song

Son of God

I search from time to time for some small blueflame remnant of a beginning lit in
the cool gloom of a diva's smoky song

I pray to saints whose names change every day who scream from the slumped
bodies of one-time soldiers

I march with unknown faces singing as though I were free

I shout at the oceans until the right word makes them bloat and swell

I talk and talk and talk and never ever tell the truth so help me Me

I wonder about the bruises on my arm the next morning

I count the brake lights stalled on the turnpike wound from north to south like a
titan's tail

I shiver my hand over the slight bend of a woman's back

I forget her name

Sometimes I wander through my own house as though I'd never seen it before
then write a clean word in the windows' grime

I play a busted up piano and sing with someone else's voice You don't know
what love is until you've learned the meaning of the blues

And I moan when I am not alone

And I somehow remember her name

And I watch the sun set every dusk through the holes in my feet

Instructions on the Painting of the Portrait of My Mother

She was swift with a knife: cold
raw chicken quartered and boned

(She learned to blood-let hens
in a barangay of Sto. Tomás)

When she'd swing precise
the butcher's blade from ear

to chopping block
the kitchen's floorboards trembled

Every evening at the same hour:
the first crack gunshot sharp

a downbeat coxswain steady
You wouldn't have thought this woman

needed comfort Even if you were her son
—lounged on the couch—the fourth-

quarter no-huddle offense wouldn't even
rouse you out of your drowse The sweet

convections of soy sauce vinegar garlic
a pot of rice on low flame—

even if you were someone else
you might mistake the clank of plate

and forks for music Still you'll render
none of this You have to paint her

sleeping You have to let us know it is late
in the evening: a rosary tangled

in her fingers how they count
each bead The faint lavender ache

of a vein Each knuckle's ridge Muscle
under mottled flesh Paint please

with care her hands Their expert work
at killing time

Photo of My Grandmother Running Toward Us on a Beach in Ilokos

Consider how happy she is
carrying the whole load of an ocean

on her head the way some women carry
water or fruits or fish My Lola

and the whole goddamned ocean
Tides Whalebone Reef And my dark

dark cousins stomping through the breakers
She is closing her eyes running

toward her American grandchildren
who wait for her on the shore

She is sopping wet trying to balance
an entire sea on her head Her arms are

flung wide open And she laughs
as if she were asking us

to bring our burdens too

Notes

"A Poet Visits With Prisoners" and "Greed" are my original lines from a larger collaborative effort with Oliver de la Paz, Aimee Nezhukumatathil, Sarah Gambito, Joseph Legaspi, Barbara Jane Reyes, and Jon Pineda.

"Kundiman Ending on a Theme from T La Rock" makes reference to the pre-Hispanic form of writing in the Philippines known as alibata.

"Poem for My Extra Nipple" was written after "Poem for My Navel" by Joseph Legaspi.

"As Glass" makes reference to lunfardo, an Argentinean street slang associated with tango music.